Praise for Joh
MAMBO

"Fierce and funny . . . Sentiment doesn't get within an arm's reach of the characterization, and yet . . . Leguizamo allows you glimpses of a heart still capable of tenderness."
—*The New York Times*

"Leguizamo's seven Latin portraits, which might, in another performer's hands, have been mere acting exercises, are shaped pieces of writing: moody, ambivalent, stunningly detailed. . . . His acting is as electric as his prose. He's a remarkable new talent."
—*The Village Voice*

"Alternately hilarious and poignant . . . [Goes] beyond light-hearted satire to probe the self-hatred of the marginalized."
—*Elle*

"Skits is the wrong word for these scenes . . . for the most part they dig deeper than that, burnt with an etching acid that might have been dished from the bathtub of Manny, Leguizamo's Puerto Rican transvestite hooker."
—*New York Post*

"Extraordinary . . . Peopled with Latino characters whose very familiarity is shockingly fresh and affecting."
—*Mirabella*

"This is savage stuff, but also very funny and exceptionally performed. . . . Leguizamo's humor is captivating because he creates characters that are both human and true."
—New York *Daily News*

"As exciting as Mardi Gras and the Fourth of July rolled into one exploding talent. . . . [Leguizamo] is a writer of enormous depth, sensitivity and detail that make his characters at once familiar and stunningly original."
—*New York Law Journal*

MAMBO MOUTH

a savage comedy by john leguizamo

BANTAM BOOKS
New York / Toronto / London
Sydney / Auckland

MAMBO MOUTH
A Bantam Book / September 1993

Library of Congress Cataloging-in-Publication Data
Leguizamo, John.
  Mambo mouth : a savage comedy / John Leguizamo.
    p.   cm.
  ISBN 0-553-37087-1
  1. Hispanic Americans—Drama.   I. Title.
PS3562.E424M35   1993
812'.54—dc20   93-9783
                                                            CIP

Published simultaneously in the United States and Canada

PRINTED IN THE UNITED STATES OF AMERICA

FFG   0   9   8   7   6   5   4   3   2   1

PRODUCTION NOTES

This text of **Mambo Mouth** is based on the original one-man show performed by John Leguizamo. **Mambo Mouth** was first produced, but not in its entirety, at the H.O.M.E. for Contemporary Theatre and Art on October 26, 1990, then mounted at The American Place Theatre's Sub-Plot Theatre on November 8, 1990. It moved to the Main Stage at the American Place on February 15, 1991. It moved again and for the last time to the Orpheum on June 2, 1991, and closed August 25, 1991.

H.O.M.E. for Contemporary Theatre and Art
DIRECTOR—Peter Askin
COSTUME CHANGES—Theresa Tetley

American Place Sub-Plot
DIRECTOR—Peter Askin
LIGHTING DESIGN—Graeme F. McDonnell
STAGE MANAGER—Joseph A. Onorato
SILHOUETTE—Theresa Tetley
SOUND DESIGN—Bruce Elman
SET DESIGN—Greg Erbach

American Place Main Stage

DIRECTOR—Peter Askin

SET DESIGN—Philipp Jung

SOUND DESIGN—Bruce Elman

MUSIC SUPERVISOR—JellyBean Benitez

COSTUME QUICK CHANGE—Theresa Tetley

PRODUCER—Wynn Handman

STAGE MANAGER—Michael Robin

Orpheum

PRODUCER—Island Visual Arts

LIGHTING DESIGN—Natasha Katz

SET DESIGN—Philipp Jung

STAGE MANAGER—Joseph A. Onorato

SILHOUETTE—Theresa Tetley

MUSIC SUPERVISOR—JellyBean Benitez

SOUND DESIGN—Bruce Elman

Mucho special thanx goes out to: Peter Askin, for being such a talented bud; Wynn Handman, for being a national treasure; David Rothenberg, for believing; Luz M. Leguizamo, for putting up with me; Sergio Leguizamo, for giving in to; Michael Bregman, for sticking up for; David Lewis, for figuring out how to; Theresa Tetley, for congeniality while under pressure; Island Records, for financing; and a special shout goes out to: Liz Heller; Mark Groubert; David Klingman; David B. Richards; Stephen Holden; Laurie Stone; Gina Velasquez Healy; Linda Gross; Juliet Wentworth; Judy Yip; Kim Merrill Askin, for giving up her honeymoon; Carolyn McDermott for letting me be crazy; Randy Rollison, H.O.M.E. for Contemporary Theatre; Mark Russell, P.S. 122; Mirtha Gregory; Angelo Parra, Jr.; Lapacazo Sandoval; Kate Lanier; Charlotte Rapisarda; Kevin Gregory; Angela Rodriguez; Dixon Place; Garage; Max Ferra, INTAR; Marshall Purdy; Michael Robin; Joe Onorato; Jeffrey Arsenault; Roxanne Laham; David Hughes; Eric Leonard; and friends, and friends of friends who sat through long, slow, unfunny, and uncatered evenings with no air-conditioning and many an insistence from me that "Hey, it will work. Shut up! I know what I'm doing. If you don't think so then you write it."

Peace

This book is for all the Latino people
who have had a hard time holding on to a dream
and just made do.

contents

p r e f a c e

I met John Leguizamo on a Wednesday afternoon when I
was auditioning twelve prospective students for my acting
class. He performed a monologue from a war movie, and my
inner Geiger counter immediately told me: "This is an
extraordinary acting talent." I accepted him in my class with
the expectancy of assigning a scene and a partner to begin the
usual process of training. But he surprised me by bringing in a
piece he had written. He was inspired by *Drinking in America,*
a collection of dramatic monologues I had directed that was
written and performed by Eric Bogosian at The American
Place Theatre. John's character was a young man trying to get
back in his girlfriend's good graces after she had locked him
out of her house. While amusing and well acted, the situation
and character were too limited to warrant further
development; I suggested that he create another character. He
later said, "I was encouraged, I made the old guy laugh."

He continually astonished the class and me with the vivid
life he gave to an assortment of Latino characters who were
ironic, multidimensional, and daring. My studio became
populated with a transvestite, an illegal alien, a hardworking

parent, a talk show host, and others . . . each a full rendition with sound, props, complete costume. Most important, each was honestly felt and accurately observed, coming from a deep organic source and always informed by an incredibly high intelligence.

John felt the freedom to share the characters with the class in early rough-draft versions—sometimes too long, sometimes not yet fully developed or shaped. Through a process involving improvising and directorial notes, the characters were brought to fuller realization. The laughter triggered by that first piece eventually turned into cheers and strong applause from my class. This was more than encouragement from his peers, it was deep admiration. We had seen the maturing of a really first-rate talent.

John has determination equal to all his other attributes, and he soon, quite logically, found places to try out his characters around New York. The favorable reception was no surprise. We had room at The American Place Theatre to do the piece on a series of weekends in our small Sub-Plot Theatre. I suggested that Peter Askin, one of my directing students, get to know John and his work. Peter was enthusiastic, and the relationship seemed promising, so we moved ahead. Their collaboration eventually took the shape of *Mambo Mouth,* which opened on November 8, 1990. The demand for tickets was so great that on February 15, 1991 we moved the show to our large theatre. What began as classroom exercises blossomed into a full-fledged off-Broadway hit.

WYNN HANDMAN

Wynn Handman is both a distinguished acting teacher and director of The American Place Theatre in New York City, which he cofounded in 1963. His role in the theater since then has been to seek out, encourage, train, and present new, exciting writing and acting talent. At The American Place Theatre, several hundred productions of new plays by living American playwrights have advanced theater culture and have been reproduced at other theaters and on television and film. Always devoted to development, The American Place Theatre has produced the early work of many important contemporary playwrights, covering a broad spectrum of styles and ethnic origins.

Since the time he taught at The Neighborhood Playhouse School of the Theatre in New York, Wynn Handman has made an important contribution to the training of actors. In more than forty years of teaching, he has trained many outstanding actors, including James Caan, Michael Douglas, Sandy Duncan, Mia Farrow, Richard Gere, Cliff Gorman, Joel Grey, Raul Julia, Margot Kidder, Frank Langella, Burt Reynolds, Tony Roberts, Christopher Walken, Denzel Washington, and Joanne Woodward, as well as hundreds of others appearing in all media. Wynn Handman has also taught at the Yale School of Drama and is the editor of Modern American Scenes for Student Actors.

preface

The first thing one notices after a few days work with John Leguizamo, aside from his obvious gifts as an actor, is that he never stops writing. For a director and collaborator this is both blessing and curse. It is a luxury to have ample material to choose from, especially when it is usually strong stuff, funny, touching, raw, unexpectedly poetic—but when it never stops, slipping under your door at three A.M., burying your desk, invading your personal life, your dreams, accompanying you on your honeymoon . . . well, we all have to make sacrifices for our art. Or our John.

Our collaboration began in June 1990, when Wynn Handman invited me to workshop *Mambo Mouth* with John in preparation for its November production at The American Place Theatre. Sitting in an audience of mostly family and friends well acquainted with his work (a developmental technique that John relies on), I watched a run-through of the monologues, some of which, like "Loco Louie," "Pepe," and "Manny the Fanny," were already substantially developed. Other characters performed that night were subsequently dropped or incorporated into other monologues.

Even at that early stage, John enhanced his performance with costumes as well as the use of slides for "Crossover King." It is evident, I think, to anyone familiar with his work, that John could have performed *Mambo Mouth* in a T-shirt and jeans with wonderful results, and some felt that the elaborate costumes would detract from John's acting virtuosity. As for the comedic effect of the slides, one had only to be in the American Place audience the night the slide projector bulb burned out and witness John describe twelve *imaginary* slides with side-splitting results to know that the slide show, like the costumes, was only an option, not a necessity.

The summer was devoted to working on the text of *Mambo Mouth,* with September reserved for rehearsal of the play for a production at H.O.M.E., a small SoHo theater, the first week of October. Collaboration on the text went something like this:

MONDAY: We work on incorporating our favorite sections of an early monologue, "Tito Testosterones," into "Agamemnon" because of their similarities. John adds two jokes to "Loco Louie," three to "Manny the Fanny," and we review slides for "Crossover King." They are all used for comic effect and we have a great time laughing at them. Later, I realize that some of them are pictures of John's family. I make a note to watch my back.

TUESDAY: John arrives with new drafts of both "Tito" and "Agamemnon," four new jokes for "Loco," a totally new (at least to me) monologue about a bouncer, and we laugh at more slides for "Crossover King." He asks if I am photogenic.

WEDNESDAY: The monologue about the bouncer has now insinuated its way into "Angel," and along with six new jokes for "Loco" comes yet another new monologue about an Astor Place drifter selling dreams. This evolved into "Inca Prince," *Mambo Mouth*'s prodigal child, because it always promised more than it delivered. Its theme, the relationship between a failed father and his shamed son, was of particular interest to us both, only increasing our frustration that we could not get it right. Although "Inca Prince" was performed most of the time on stage, it was cut from HBO's presentation.

THURSDAY: John is filming *Hangin' with the Homeboys,* giving me time to concentrate on the same material two days running. There is a God!

FRIDAY: John returns with more new material. Where did he find the time? I am giddy with the news that John habitually writes until four A.M. If there is a God, She's at John's place, swapping material.

Variations of this schedule continued all summer. As September approached, deadlines to freeze the text were made and broken, then made again. I was learning that John's theatrical trunk held a world of characters, stories, and jokes developed over years of stand-up and improvisational work, and he *never* discarded material, especially if it had ever gotten a laugh.

And though the stories might change, it seemed as if he had known the characters like family for years. He could inhabit them at will, never concerned with making them likable, only truthful, instinctively aware that empathy, not sympathy, is the ultimate test of a character's universality.

John makes strong, often extreme choices in his writing as well as his acting, and rehearsals continued to explore the text, forcing the braggadocio of Agamemnon, Angel, and Loco Louie to the moment when a sudden glimpse of vulnerability stripped them bare. Agamemnon reduced to a Cuban cabana boy sweeping the sand; Angel finally forced to turn to his mother for help in front of the cops, and being refused; Loco Louie, unable to admit that his first sexual experience left him with questions not answers; Manny, the girlfriend from hell, taking charge of her life with the help of some Krazy Glue; Pepe, the illegal alien, giving voice to the silent minority of American citizens who are treated worse than illegal aliens; and the Crossover King, preaching the gospel of living a lie and at the same time hilariously incapable of following his own advice.

The October workshop at H.O.M.E. provided more opportunities to tighten the material, locate the unseen characters, find opportunities to interact with the audience ("Agamemnon," "Manny the Fanny," and "Crossover King"), experiment with the order of the monologues, and sharpen the costume changes. This last was critical to the pace of the show, and by the time *Mambo Mouth* reached the American Place, John and Theresa Tetley, his expert costume-changer, had the complicated changes down to a minute. The backstage intervals were initially accompanied by music, which was from the outset an important element of *Mambo Mouth*. Most characters entered and exited to music, and some (Agamemnon, Loco Louie, and Manny) danced as well as sang. To further tighten the interludes, we experimented with beginning the monologues backstage while John changed costumes. That idea was expanded to include a character continuing his monologue after his exit. Music, sound effects, dialogue, naked body parts, the backstage circus life of *Mambo Mouth*, became far too interesting to hide. With the American Place production, John began changing behind a scrim, and with Theresa exuberantly playing a number of roles (the cop who wallops Angel, Inca Prince's bickering wife, the maître d' who throws Manny out of the restaurant), their silhouettes extended the onstage life of one monologue even as John prepared for another. By moving closer or farther away from the scrim as well as adding lights and rear-projected slides, the audience was invited to imagine a world of *Mambo Mouth* that extended beyond the stage.

Mambo Mouth played for over nine months on four different stages, and during the entire run John continued to tinker with his writing and performance. When new material didn't fit existing characters, new characters began to form. The Gigante family, featured in *Spic-O-Rama,* began popping up in performance spaces downtown. Trusted family and friends, all astute directors and critics of John's work, began the developmental process again. Happily, so did I.

PETER ASKIN

Peter Askin most recently directed Spic-O-Rama *for broadcast on Home Box Office, and onstage both in New York and at the Goodman Theatre in Chicago. Off-Broadway credits include* Mambo Mouth, Reality Ranch, Beauty Marks, Ourselves Alone, Reno, *and the New York and Los Angeles premiers of* Down an Alley Filled with Cats. *He has written for film (*Smithereens, Old Scores, Seasons Greetings, Selling Kate*), television (*WNET's Bet One I Make It*), and print (*The New York Times *and* Life *magazine). He has collaborated with John Leguizamo on a television comedy special and a new screenplay,* White Chocolate. *Peter Askin is married to actress/playwright Kim Merrill, and is the director of the Westside Theatre in New York City.*

introduction

I was born in Latin America. I had to—my mother was there. But I came of age in the land that time forgot: Jackson Heights, Queens, the truest melting pot of New York City. It's a modern-day Ellis Island. All the peoples of the world stop there before they go on to wherever it is they have to go—Irish, Italians, Jews, Puerto Ricans, Dominicans, Chinese, Greeks, Colombians, Ecuadorians, and every possible combination thereof.

My upbringing is probably most remarkable for its transitions, and in many ways change has been the leitmotiv of my life ever since. We were constantly moving, so I went to a different school every year. Every year I had to make new friends and get used to new faces, new bullies, new girls, and new teachers. I lived in Bogotá, Colombia, till I was five; then Jackson Heights, Elmhurst, east Elmhurst, Astoria, and Jamaica, Queens; Manhattan's East Village, West Village, uptown, downtown, and midtown. Pick any of the many armpits of New York, and I've lived there.

My parents kept moving, but I found them. They were trying to Jones-up, to fulfill the immigrants' dream of improving their life-style. We started in a studio apartment with a Murphy bed, which seemed like sci-fi from my third-world point of view. We then moved to a one-bedroom apartment, then to a first-floor apartment with a backyard, and finally to our own house. Unfortunately, all the rooms but one were rented out, so we had to live as if we were in a studio again.

I have one brother, on whom I inflicted all sorts of torture. I was a mad Frankenstein and he was my monster. I often made him taste things no human being has ever tasted—or ever will. How many times did I pull his bathing suit down at Astoria Pool? How many times did I try to smother him under a pillow just to get something happening on a dull Sunday? Too often! Luckily for me, I was the elder brother, so there was no one to torture me—except my father.

When I say my father was a strict autocratic-totalitarian-despotic-dictator-disciplinarian, I don't mean that in a negative way. He was in love with culture, the word *culture*. He wanted everything to smack of taste and decency, so he smacked culture into my brother and beat the fear of God into me. He did this to show the world we weren't just *any* immigrant Hispanic family just off the boat. His boys knew Puccini and Matisse; we were classy.

In his youth my father studied film. When he was nineteen he fell in love with Italian neo-realism and decided he wanted to be a director. So he studied for two years at Cinecittà, one of the great filmmaking studios in Italy. Family lore has it he mind-melded with Fellini while both imbibed at the local trattoria. He returned to Bogotá when he was twenty-one and immediately started a family. Having to bring home the Kraft macaroni and cheese put an end to my father's cinematic aspirations, but you could say I'm continuing the family tradition.

My mom is a very attractive and exotic (euphemism for

ethnic-looking) woman. She's part Native American, part Arab, part Spaniard, and rumors pervade of Jewish and African contributions as well. She could have had any man in greater Bogotá, but chose my dad because he had that cosmopolitan Euro flair.

Growing up in Queens was a great education in comedy and survival. Unlike the other boroughs, gangs in Queens did not force you to participate; membership was voluntary. In the Bronx, Brooklyn, and Manhattan, you either had to join or become a target. I used to visit my cousin in Spanish Harlem. There I'd find all the romance a ten-year-old could wish for: tough gangs, pretty girls, great parties. Sex was in the air, and so was fast living. In Queens we had gangs like the Spiral Sisters—Catholic-school girls who beat up boys in younger grades—while Manhattan had the Tomahawks and Savage Skulls, who'd beat up anyone, regardless of age, sex, or religious or political inclination.

I got arrested a few times, but only for stupid things: once for truancy, once for going off on a cop (always a big-mouth, I wouldn't let him have the last word), and once for breaking into a subway conductor's booth with a friend and commandeering the intercom. Some of my friends were in deeper trouble with the law for stealing cars and for dealing drugs. I wasn't that wild, but I always wanted to hang out with the really cool, hardened street fighters. I was a gangster wannabe.

At about that time I was voted Most Talkative in high school. (I wasn't politically organized enough to win Most Funny.) I spent most of tenth grade in the dean's office, inventing excuses and promising to mend my evil ways. My English teacher, Miss Ross, and my history teacher, Miss Singer, encouraged my performance ability subliminally by allowing me to wreak havoc in their classrooms. But it was my math teacher, Mr. Zufa, who actually suggested I take up comedy. The idea of studying acting sounded good to me, so I went to the Yellow Pages and looked up drama schools. I first tried out Sylvia Leigh's Showcase Theater. Sylvia Leigh thought she was Blanche DuBois. She had an affected accent and was always dimming the lights around her. She had us do lots of speech exercises and script analysis.

My first acting-school scene was an Oscar-award performance if I do say so myself: *Dino*, the wiry troubled street youth—Sal Mineo had done it as a teleplay. I then got offers from New York University student filmmakers, who in my mind had the stature of Coppola. But after that initial success, my performances at the school sucked. "How?" you ask? Don't ask! Let's just say I've been chasing that high ever since.

At this point I realized a successful acting career requires serious commitment, so I decided to become a student-aholic. I studied my craft at NYU, the Strasberg Institute, HB Studio, and with Ken Eulo. Finally, I was cast in the starring role of a critically acclaimed student film called *Five Out of Six*. That got me an audition for *Miami Vice*, where I had a recurring role as a cocaine Mafia prince. If there had been an acting police on *Miami Vice*, I would've been arrested on too many counts. Then I was in two plays at The Public Theater in the East Village. Joseph Papp would tutor me in Shakespearean pentameter before my entrance as Puck. But I felt Puck to be too confining for my acting style. So I went wild. And I'm certain my unique interpretation destroyed *A Midsummer Night's Dream* for many a neophyte. Sorry, Bill.

From there followed a string of movie roles, playing the drug pusher/terrorist/immigrant/gigolo stereotype Latino: in *Revenge* I'm a gun-toting Mexican lackey; in *Die-Hard 2* I'm a subliminal terrorist—you have to freeze-frame to catch what's left of me post editing; in *Regarding Henry* I'm the mugger. I have particularly fond memories of my first big film,

Casualties of War, in which I played the silent minority—and I do mean silent! As the token Hispanic, I had very few lines and was meant to be part of the background. Instead, I gave the best face-gesticulating performance of my life. Fortunately, Brian De Palma never caught me enlarging my role, so I got away with it.

In the meantime, I was writing jokes for a children's theater company called the Off-Center Theatre, trying to juice up my parts in the various children's classics they presented. My Jack in the Beanstalk was a scam artist who tried to rip off the giant by making him shoot craps for the goose, play three-card monte for the harp, and toss a coin for his wife. Either the children were bused to the theater or the company traveled to Harlem and Spanish Harlem to perform in public schools and community centers. It was the highlight of my life. No other acting job, before or since, has given me so much satisfaction. The kids enjoyed it almost as much as I did. Inspired by their honest and uninhibited responses, I couldn't control myself and ended up stealing every scene.

I then joined the improv group First Amendment for a stint and found out that most improv is *not* improv, but sort of a script with a lot of blanks. Around this time I began serious work on my first one-man play. I performed twenty-minute pieces at legendary performance art spaces: P.S. 122, Dixon Place, and the Comedy Cellar. I took the point of view of what would have happned if Hispanics had a hand in history. I did a detective story with a Latino shamus hunting down the murderer of the Messiah. The Lord had been done in by the Mob because he was muscling in on their territory. He wanted to take gambling out of the temples and get rid of Mary Magdalene's pimp. He was getting wine from stones and not giving the Organization a percentage. So the gumshoe goes to Long Island and talks to Joseph and Mary Cohen. Then he goes down to Little Italy and talks to some wise guys till he meets up with Judas who has a contract out for him. They shoot it out and, of course, our hero wins and lives. There are eight million stories in New York and this has been one of them. The reception was overwhelming. I knew I had found myself, had arrived into my own. After a few more forgotten films, *Mambo Mouth* was conceived, and the rest is history—or press.

Mambo Mouth came to me as I was fighting very strenuously with my girlfriend of the moment back in August 1989. Adversity is my inspiration. I wrote the pieces, tried them out in the clubs downtown, and then took them to Wynn Handman, who was instrumental in my believing in my work. He helped me shape the pieces and then did the greatest thing ever: He introduced me to Peter Askin, the Scorsese to my De Niro.

Mambo Mouth is a combination cathartic purge of popular Latin media-types and my own personal take on street prototypes and wannabes. Some reviewers and members of the press insinuated that I was perpetuating stereotypes rather than lambasting them. I'm not going to defend my work because it's not my job—it's my mother's. But if my years of performing comedy have taught me anything, it's that you've got to be strong to make fun of yourself. In creating *Mambo Mouth,* I felt that mocking the Latin community was one of the most radical ways to empower it. I love the world I come from, and only because I do can I poke fun at it. Like Latin life itself, *Mambo Mouth* is harsh, graphic, funny—and at the same time tragic, desperate, and painfully raw. No stereotype could contain the pressure of all those explosive, conflicting emotions.

But enough about me. Now read my work.

glossary
of foreign terms

adiós: good-bye; later
arrigato: (Japanese) thank you
arroz con pollo circuit: chicken and rice circuit
arroz con pollo thighs: chicken and rice thighs
Ay, coño!: Oh, damn!
Ay coño, yo quiero perder control, ser lo que soy, ayudame, mamacita, estoy jodido, quiero bailar y gozar.: Oh damn, I want to lose control, be wild, help me, mommy, I'm fucked, I want to dance and have fun.
Ay, Dios mío de misericordia, mi culpa.: Oh! God of mercy, my fault.
Ay, fo: Euuu, yuck, eekie, poo, nasty
Ay, gracias, Papi! Gracias!: Oh! Thank you, darling! Thanks!
Ay, he was bien de groovy, tú sabes? Casi que me muero.: Damn, he was very groovy, you know? To die for.
Ay, mira, precioso: Hey, look, precious
Ay, Perdóna.: Damn! I'm sorry.
baboso: drooler, slimy

bendito: poor thing

bizcocho: pussy, beaver

bodega: grocery store

bruto: stupid

bubeleh: (Yiddish) Term of endearment meaning darling, honey, sweetheart, little doll.

cabeza: head

cabrón: bastard

cabrón, idiota, medio-malparido, cagado, pedazo de mierda envuelto, baboso, bobo: bastard, idiot, blue baby, dirty butt, wrapped-up piece of shit, drooler, dope

católico: Catholic

Chaito, señor policía: Good-bye, Mr. Policeman.

chucawala: (Chicanoism) baby daughter

cocotazo: noogie

cojones: balls

coño: our equivalent of *damn* and has as many meanings

coño imbécil: damn imbecile

cuchifrito: deep-fried turnovers

culo: ass; butt; rump

desgraciado: ungrateful (but stronger)

desgraciado, bruto pendejo, que nunca sirvió para nada: ungrateful, stupid dummy, that never did anything worthwhile

Dozo ohairi kudusai: (Japanese) Please come in.

el mundo de "cheap thrills y expensive regrets": the world of cheap thrills and expensive regrets

en la otra: in the other

ése: (Chicanoism) meaning dude; bud; guy; fellow; homey

gracias: thank you

Gracias, chico: Thanks, kid.

Gracias, pendejita.: Thank you, little dummy.

Hai!: (Japanese) Yes; uh-huh; I hear ya.

Hasta la próxima. Epa!: Until the next time. Funky!

hermanos: brothers

hijo de puta: son of a whore

Hola, Abuelita: What's up, Grandma?

Hola! Epa!: (said while dancing) Wow! Funky! Groovy!

Hola, Mamá, cómo esta?: What's up, moms? How's things?

Hola, Negrito.: What's up, my little dark one?

Hola, Ramón!: Hey, Ramon!

idiota: (this one is obvious) idiot

In your culo, puto maricón sucio: In your ass, dirty faggot
    fucker

kibitzing: (Yiddish) to putz around

kine-ahora: (Yiddish) Expression used to show one's praises
    are genuine and not contaminated by envy.

Konichi-wa: (Japanese) Hello.

Latina puta-bitch: Latina whore-bitch

Los latinos debemos ser unidos y jamás seremos vencidos.:
    Latinos united, we'll never be divided.

mamis: babes; foxes; honeys; chicks

manos en la caca: hands in the shit

Mazel tov: (Yiddish) Good luck.

Mi culpa, señor. Que sufrimiento, ay!: My fault, lord. What
    suffering, oh!

mija: my daughter, my darling

mijo: my son, my darling

mira: look

Mira, mira! Policía, policía, please! Ayuda, socorro, socorro!:
    Look, hey! Police, police, please! Help, save me, save me!

Miss Masoquista: Miss Masochist

Ms. Caca de Toro: Ms. Bullshit

Nada. Bruto pendejo idiota: Nothing. Stupid, dummy, idiot

nena: girlfriend

No más, no más: No more, no more (Duran said this once
    before being pummeled by Sugar Ray)

número uno: number one

Olé!: Spanish expletive meaning something like Way to go!

Orale!: (Chicanoism) What's up?

Orale, gabacho pendejo: Waz up, dumb whitey?

Pa' fuera, pa' fuera, sucio demonio, coco inmundo, ayudame Diosito!: Get out, get out, dirty demon, heinous bogeyman, help me my little Lord!

papi: daddy; baby; honey

pendejo: dummy (masculine); sometimes means pubic hair

Perdóna, señor policía.: I'm sorry, Mr. Policeman.

pinga: dick; johnson; love stick; tube steak; hot beef injection

pipi: dick; weeny; wee-wee

Presentado por Telemundo de Paterson, New Jersey: Presented by Teleworld from Paterson, New Jersey

primo: cousin

Primo, por favor dejeme ir que somos de la mismita sangre.: Cuz, please let me go, we are of the same blood.

puto: fucker

Qué te pasó?: What happened to you?

santero: a witch doctor or shaman of disputable powers; Santeria is a religious practice in Latin countries taken from African voodoo, native South American folklore, and European Catholicism

santero mágico: magic man

Sayonara: (Japanese) Good-bye.

Se me paró!: Popped a woody!; Pop-up tent in my pants!: I got a hard-on!

Shitsurei: (Japanese) Excuse me.

shmoozing: (Yiddish) rumors; idle talk; heart to heart prolonged talk; gossip

"Sueños Calientes de Noches Frías y Pecados Católicos": "Hot Dreams of Catholic Sins on Cold Nights"

También presentado por Wine Cooler Sangría. La bebida preferida pro los latinos de los nineties. El sabor del Caribe. Rico. Sauve.: Also presented by Wine Cooler

Blood-drink. The preferred drink by the Latinos of the nineties. The taste of the Caribbean. Tasty. Smooth.

Te lo corto!: I'll cut it off!

tetas: tits; mammaries; breasts; jammies; jugs

tortilla: Mexican pancakes

Tú eres mi moreno, mi macho.: You are my brown one, my main man.

Tú eres un mugre, un moco, una cucaracha.: You are dirt, a booger, a roach.

Yo te conozco.: I know you.

Yo te quiero.: I love you.

glossary
of slang terms

buggin': losing it; going out of your mind; going crazy
crazy: an adjective denoting greatness
dissin': disrespecting
dope: great, awesome
dufus: dolt; big gangly one; goofy person
five-finger discount: stolen
flex: to use force; show off power
frontin': putting up a front; posing
goofin': just kidding, joking
ho: whore
ill: when something is very cool
motha: short for motherfucker
sweatin': bothering; having the hots for someone; on
    someone's jock

"Life is a dream." —*Calderon*

"I want to be
like the waves on the sea,
like the clouds in the wind,
but I'm me.
One day I'll jump
out of my skin.
I'll shake the sky
like a hundred violins." —*Sandra Cisneros*

"Olive skin makes good kin." —*M*A*S*H*

AGAMEMNON

(Offstage: Agamemnon sings "Strangers in the Night.")
STAGE MANAGER: Yo, Mr. Agamemnon, you're live in thirty seconds.

(A robed Agamemnon enters from the back of the house and crosses onto the stage.)
AGAMEMNON: Coño, desgraciado, bruto pendejo, idiota!

Mr. Producer? Mr. Producer? I'm not going on. I refuse to go on. You know why? Because some unemployed actor is still in my dressing room. How do you expect me to prepare? I had to go into the alley, and this undesirable element—my wife—tried to talk to me. I need to visualize and concentrate because I am a method talk-show host.

Okay, okay. You don't have to get somebody else. I guess since you people came to see me, I owe you something.

(Preparation very dramatic.) Ay, Dios mío de misericordia, mi culpa. Mi culpa, señor. Que sufrimiento, ay! I am king of the Amazon jungle. *(Jungle sounds.)* Oooh, ooh, ooh, ooh! Aah, aah, aah, aah! *(Maniacal laughter, then*

hysterical crying.) I can't do it, Mr. Producer. I don't feel it. You know, we are supposed to be a team, working for me, the star. It's just like my uncle Segismundo used to say: "The whole is the sum of the parts—and some of the parts don't seem to be working."

Difficult? Now you're calling me names? *(To audience:)* People, am I difficult? *(Waits for lukewarm response.)* Well, I must be then. You all sure are uppity for Off-Broadway prices. But people, I'm sorry you had to witness this debacle, but some people think they can treat me like a second-class citizen, like I'm some kind of Third World idiot, but what they don't realize is that I built myself from the arroz con pollo circuit to what I am today. And now HBO is here, and I'm moving my show right out of this pathetic little theater. Don't try to apologize now, desgraciado.

(Moves to stage rear and takes off robe, revealing leopard jockeys.) Can I have a little privacy? I feel naked. *(Flexes as scrim descends. To silhouetted figure who appears to aid in dressing:)* Where have you been? Shmoozing and kibitzing again?

(Comes back around scrim. To audience:) And people, please don't sit on your hands tonight. God gave them to you for a reason. Use them. Gracias. *(Ducks back behind scrim until applause dies. Reappears.)* I didn't say stop, did I? *(Ducks behind scrim.)* The more you give, the more you get! Well, I guess you're not going to get anything. Recession-type audience.

STAGE MANAGER: Five . . . four . . . three . . . two . . . Agamemnon, you're live!

(Stage lights up, Agamemnon strides forward. He is dressed in a snazzy white suit, floral silk shirt unbuttoned at the neck to reveal gold chains, a white slouch hat, and black-and-white spectator shoes. He wears a few gold rings, a gold watch, a gold hoop earring, and a pencil-thin moustache. The only props are downstage: a stool and a small table, on which are a wine cooler, a cellular phone, a letter, a cue card, and a beam-balance, shielded from view.)

Live, baby, I'm always live. *(Show's mambo theme music begins. Agamemnon signals audience to clap.)* Work with me, people. Hola! Epa! Stop it, you're spoiling me. Hola, hola, people, and welcome to *Naked Personalities*, the most dangerous show on public access TV. Where we take an uncensored look at your

most favorite celebrity—me! That's right. And
for the few of you who don't know me *(winks)*,
my name is Agamemnon Jesús Roberto Rafael
Rodrigo Papo Pablo Pacheco Pachuco del Valle
del Río del Monte del Coño de su madre
*(pauses to swig from wine cooler and signals to
cut music)* López Sánchez Rodríguez Martinez
Morales Mendoza y Mendoza.

But you can call me handsome. Why not? I
deserve it. *(Searches audience.)* You women are
probably asking yourselves, is he or isn't he?
Well yes, ladies, I am . . . married. But don't
lose hope because my lawyers are working on
it, and pretty soon I'm going to be out and
about. So beware . . . grrrrrrrr! *(Rolls r's.)*
But remember, ladies, I'm not omnipresent—
only omnipotent. Huh! *(Pelvic thrust.)*

Okay, people, I'd like to take a quick moment to say hello to all the women I have loved around the world, if you don't mind. How you doing? I miss you. 'Bye!

Okay, people. *(Puts down cooler, perches on stool.)* Let's open the show as we always do: by reading letters from women who want to be loved by me around the world. *(Picks up letter.)* And this first letter is from a woman who wants to be loved by me in El Salvador. Nice little underdeveloped country.

And it says: "Dear Mr. Agamemnon"—she respects me—"I am a Republican, single, Hispanic woman. Please come to my rescue. Invade me. Blockade me. Dick—tate me." *(To audience, pointing at letter:)* I didn't see that the line continued. "Spill your oils on my virginal beaches. Deplete me of my natural resources." Grrrrrrrr! "Be mine forever. Yours in Christ, Mimosa."

(Rises from stool, walks downstage. Pulls silver cigarette case out of pocket and removes cigarette, with flair, as he speaks.) Well, let's get something straight right off the top, okay, Mimosa? I don't get involved with my women. I'm a short-term guy. I don't fall in love, and

I certainly won't marry you. *(Pulls silver lighter from pocket, flicks it open, and lights it across his thigh. Casually brings flame to cigarette.)* The only thing you can count on me for is satisfaction, gratification, ecstasy, passion, decadence, debauchery—and maybe kissing.

(Walks back to table and picks up another letter.) This next letter is from a woman who wants to be loved by me in Havana. That's my home town, by the way. Wait a minute—I already had her! Please, please, no repeats, ladies. No repeats on this show. *(To stage manager:)* Coño imbécil! I told you to read all my letters.

(To audience:) As a matter of fact, this Little Miss Charming here thought she was the last Coca-Cola in the desert. But people, let me tell you something—there's a difference between beauty and charm. A beautiful woman is one who I notice, but a charming woman is one who notices me.

Now we are going to start taking calls from our male viewers, so please call me on my chellular phone. Call me on the chellular because this is an opportunity for us Latino men to be vulnerable for one moment in our lives. So call me and lean your heads on my shoulder. Because that's what I'm here for. Whatever female problems you have, be it wife problems, mistress problems, two-women-at-a-time problems, prepubescent-nubile-girl problems, whatever the problem. Because if you have a woman in your life, you gotta be suffering from estrogen poisoning.

So dial 970-WEEP. This is your chance to bond and share. Come on, do two sixteen-ounce curls *(mimes weight-lifting)*, whatever it takes, and call me. I dare you. Last week I taught you how to save money by making love to yourselves. This week I'm going to teach you how to maximize your male potential with the mamis. Don't let the big cabeza tell the little cabeza what to do.

(Sips wine cooler.) Okay, first caller. You're on the air.

CALLER #1 *(voice is heard from offstage; Agamemnon listens, smoking:)* Orale! My name is Pepe, and I'm calling from Flushing.

AGAMEMNON: How ya doin', Pepe.

CALLER #1: I just want to say that I really like your show a lot.

AGAMEMNON: Gracias, chico. Gracias.

CALLER #1: My problem is that I'm dating a beautiful woman right now, and I've taken her out many times and bought her all kinds of gifts—

AGAMEMNON: You're in trouble already, my friend.

CALLER #1: We have a—what do you call it?—Christian relationship. But I want a lot more. What can you do for me?

AGAMEMNON: Pepe, you deserve a lot more. I know exactly what you are going through, because I have been there myself. This last Jezebel I was with did the exact same thing to me. I call this the Goldilocks Syndrome. That is when a fine blonde sexy mami comes into your life from nowhere, and suddenly she's eating all your food, messing up your fine upholstery, sleeping in your bed, and she's not giving you a damn thing. You got to get rid of that barracuda before she eats your heart raw.

Now let's take a look at Agamemnon's Scales of Justness. *(Reveals balance.)* Okay, Pepe, you've given her what? *(Places three weights into one pan of balance.)* Candy, flowers, and in your case, probably plastic slipcovers. And she's giving you what? *(Holds up uneven scale.)* Look at that! Nada. Bruto pendejo idiota.

You did it your way. Now do it Agamemnon's way. Take back the candy, the flowers, the plastic slipcovers. *(Removes weights from pan.)* Tell her you're going to call and don't. Mistreat her. Sleep around. *(Places all three weights in other pan of balance.)* And pretty soon those scales are gonna be on your side—okay, baby? Next caller, you're on the air.

CALLER #2: Hello, Agamemnon. My name is Angel, and I'm calling from Rikers. Yeah, I got this problem. This fine blonde sexy mami I've been getting visitation rights to isn't spending time with me anymore. She tells me that she's taking care of sick relatives, but I don't believe her. What can I do?

AGAMEMNON: Don't you ever believe them. Because I know exactly what you're going through. I have been there myself. This last piranha I was with did the exact same thing to me. I call this one the Little Red Riding Hood

Syndrome. And that is when a fine blonde sexy
mami is telling you that she's going to
Granny's, but meanwhile she's in the woods
being eaten by a wolf!

Stop being a eunuch. Get rid of her. And give
me her number—I'll take care of her my way.
Next caller, you're on the air.

CALLER #3: My name is Manny.

AGAMEMNON: Hello, sweetheart.

CALLER #3: This is a must-miss show on my
list—

AGAMEMNON: I'm sorry to hear that.

CALLER #3: —because you are a misogynistic,
homophobic, sexist, sorry sack of shit—
(Agamemnon hangs up.)

AGAMEMNON: Well, thank you, Ms. Caca de Toro, for your cojones. But people, this is nothing. I'm already used to negativity. My father, Agamemnon Senior, made sure of that. Every night before he tucked me into bed, he'd say, "Agamemnon Junior, I can't believe that out of a hundred thousand sperm, you were the quickest." Oh, my father was a great source of comfort in my life. But where are you now? Eh, Papi? They caught you with your manos en la caca, and they sent you back to Cuba, desgraciado, bruto pendejo, que nunca sirvió para nada.

(Brings stool to foot of stage.) Bring the camera in closer. Tighten up to there. That's it. *(Strikes a pose.)* For all you Pepes and Angels and all you brothers and hermanos out there—if you learn only one thing from me tonight, it is my prayer that you don't fall in love with beautiful women. It's not worth it. Go for the ugly ones, then the loss won't mean as much.

Life gives you the test and then the lesson. That's how it works. I have loved my women too much, and they abused this privilege. There was a time when my love was this raw, all-consuming, back-breaking thing. This one woman—I would walk over hot briquets for her, make love like an endangered species, fight for her, make sacrifices—but for what? For what? So that one day she could step on my gentle trusting little heart and crush it. No más, no más, those days are over. As you get older, your heart shrivels up just like your cojones.

(Notices cue from stage manager.) Do you mind? I was trying to have a moment with my brothers. *(Picks up cue card, poses for camera, and reads in booming announcer's voice.)* Naked Personalities presentado por Telemundo de Paterson, New Jersey. Paterson, New Jersey. También *(picks up wine cooler)* presentado por Wine Cooler Sangría. Wine Cooler Sangría. La bebida preferida por los latinos de los nineties! El sabor del Caribe. Rico. Suave.

(Rises from stool, walks to center stage.) Okay, people. Without much further ado, it gives me great pleasure to introduce—oh, you knew it was coming, didn't you? That's right! The cultural part of the show. Because nobody is going to leave here saying that Agamemnon is uncultured.

(Moves furniture out of the way.) I would like to do a reenactment from a major motion picture that I once did, for which I won Best New Face in a Film Not Released. Because the director, who couldn't direct traffic, was an egomaniac and also the cameraman, and he

forgot to take the cap off the lens. So all I have to show for it is my memory. *(Crushes cigarette with toe.)*

(Removes hat and gives it to silhouette dresser, upstage left.) But I'm going to give you a little taste. Or as they say in New York delis, a little schmear. *(Removes jacket and gives it to silhouette, upstage right.)* Gracias, pendejita.

It was called *(overemoting) Sueños Calientes de Noches Frías y Pecados Católicos.* Which loosely translates *Nocturnal Emissions*—I mean, *Emotions.*

Imagine this, if you will . . . *(Hums "Strangers in the Night," looks around expectantly, yells)* imagine this, if you will! *(Lighting changes.)* Gracias.

Fade in. It is Florida. The Mecca for the retired, the refugee. God's waiting room. It's hot, oh yes, very hot, and the sun is setting. And *(mimes)* strolling down Miami Beach, picking up little broken seashells, is *(rolls r's)* RRRRRRRRebecca. And she's hot too. But she's also old and leathery and wrinkly—but American, oh yes, very American.

And just like her horoscope predicted, awaits me—RRRRRRRRamón, the Cuban cabana boy. And I'm sweeping the sand *(mimes)*, closing the umbrellas. And I'm dark, devilish, desperate *(crosses himself)*, Católico, and illegal, oh yes, very illegal.

Music swells. Romance is in the air. *(Conks salsa music and dances.)* They do the dance. The "I Want Something for Nothing" dance. *(Conks and dances.)*

RRRRamón holds her age-spotted, quivering, gelatinous, buttless body in his arms. *(Mimes dancing, holding one hand upright to simulate Rebecca's face.)* She presses against his alien Amazonian manroot. *(Gyrates hips.)* She wants fulfillment. She wants sin.

Close up. *(Makes frame around face with hands.)* I am that sin. I am that forbidden, primitive, savage Caribbean lust-quencher. Extreme close up. *(Smaller hand frame. Aside:)* The camera loves me. *(Back in frame.)* She's my chance, my dream, my opportunity. *(Aside:)* My green card. *(Drops frame.)* But people, people—I know that if I unleash just one drop of my Latino man-milk, she's gonna drop me like some empty jar of Porcelana. Boom!

(Conks and dances.) So we play the cat-and-spouse game. I penetrate her—with my glare. She gives me a look that I can feel in my hip pocket. Dolly shot. *(Mimes cameraman on dolly, smoothly crossing stage, crouched low. Then returns to mime of conversation with hand as Rebecca.)* She calls me Chocolate Eyes. I call her Albino Beauty. She calls me her greasy, treacherous raven. I call her *(licks fingers and yanks her imaginary hair)* Grandmother!

She is on fire—I can feel that hot blood pounding through her varicose veins. She says to me *(Spanish spoken with tacky American accent)*, "Yo te quiero. Tú eres mi moreno, mi macho." I say to her, "Please don't ruin my language." She demands satisfaction. I hold out for authentifisicisicisication.

Oh—she is outraged! No one has ever talked to her that way. She calls me he-slut. I call her Aryan whore. She calls me ethnic beast. I call her bitch-goddess. She slaps me! *(Shrinks back.)* I kiss her. *(Kisses hand.)* She slaps me again! *(Shrinks back.)* I kiss her again. *(Kisses hand.)* She kisses me. I slap her! *(Claps hands together loudly.)*

We are at an impasse! She won't naturalize. I won't fertilize. She won't legitimate, I'm not going to consummate. Cut!

The idiota pendejo director ran out of film at that point, so I can't tell you no more. I can tell you I never got my green card. But I can also tell you that she never got any— *(Hand gestures sex.)*

(Notices stage manager signaling.) Ay, coño! That's all the time we have for today. I didn't realize—we were having such a good time. Okay, people, please join me next week when my guest is going to be a very dear close personal friend of mine—me! Oh yes, but I'm also going to have a lot of other guests who are going to talk about how talented I am. And I'm also going to do another reenactment of a major network TV series I once did that was canceled—because, people, let me tell you something. I have a lot of enemies in Hollywood. People who are jealous of my talent and my career.

Okay, okay. I'm going, I'm going. All right, people, thank you for joining me, and please don't drink and drive, okay? And please use protection. Because it is better to lose one minute of your life than to lose your life in one minute. Hasta la próxima. Epa! Huh!

(Theme song plays as Agamemnon exits upstage. Lights down.)

(Backstage lights up. Silhouetted figure dances upstage.)

LOCO LOUIE: Yo, where you going? Can I hang wich youse? . . . Come on, why not? I'm a man, man. I just got some. . . . Oh yeah? Well, your mother is so stupid that she trips over the cordless phone! . . . I didn't say nothin'. . . . Have a good one. Peace. Yeah, later.

(Stage lights up. Enter Loco Louie, a loose-limbed, hyperactive kid, around thirteen years old. He's wearing a red shortset with high-top basketball sneakers, a yellow baseball cap with the visor bent straight up, brass knuckles, a gold Batman medallion on a thick silver chain, and a gold front tooth. He's carrying a blaring boom box and groovin' to a kickin' lick.)

(Yells to a window above audience.) Yo! Chonchi! *(Puts down box, grooves some more.)* Chonchi! *(One more groove.)* Yo, smegma-breath, come down man! Come down. I got something seriously dope to tell you, boy. . . . Why not? Well, do your homework later. . . . Okay, I'll wait for you. Hurry up. *(Seriously dope moves.)*

Hey, Chonchi, man, where you been? *(Turns off music.)* I've been looking everywhere for you, tithead! I even called your house—yup, yup—and your pops said you was in the bathroom buffin' the helmet. Ahhh! Busted! Ha, ha! You got busted! Ahhh! *(Cackles.)* Chill, I'm just goofin' wichoo. You buggin' and all that. Step off, Chonchi. Just step off.

Okay, look me up and down and see if you notice anything particularly different about me today. Take your time. Just look me up and down. *(Strikes homeboy gangster poses.)* What are you, blind or what, pendejo? I'm a man, man! Yup, I just got some! Ahhh! Go Loco! Go Loco! Go Loco! Go Loco! *(Serious dope groove.)*

Here comes Shanté, man. Let me do the talking, all right?

(Calls out to woman passing downstage.) Hey, yo, Mami! *(Kiss.)* How about a little tongue drill? *(Rolls out tongue and flicks it ferociously. She ignores him.)* Dyke!

(To Chonchi:) So where was I? Oh yeah—so check this out. I'm hanging by my lonesome, playing some hoops and shit, right? When Ninja comes along, and he's got this big box of caffeine pills that he got on a five-finger discount. And he tells me that it gives you the strength of ten men—if you know my meaning? You know my meaning! So I pop fifteen of those suckers right away, right? And I never even had coffee and shit.

So we're waiting for the shit to kick in, right? *(Whistles.)* And then one, two, three—*(Goes rigid.)* We are human hard-ons. We are horny as shit, boy. All we can think about is fucking. All we can talk about is fucking. We are fucked. So we say, "Fuck it, let's go fuck!"

So what do we do? We jets over to Nilda's Bodega and Bordello. We had to, 'cause all this has been buildin' inside us since we were born, and we can't get any to save our lives—and it hurts. Uh-unh, it ain't for lack of trying. You know me, Chonchi—I don't limit myself to things that breathe. Word! *(Bugs.)*

So we gets there, and we ring. *(Mimes ringing doorbell, makes buzzer sound.)* Nothing. So we rings again—nothing again. So we rings some more . . . nothing some more. So we figure they're sold out, right? But as we start to step, this big pockmarked, bald-headed, bad-breathed— *(Covers his mouth.)* Say it, don't spray it. I want the news, not the weather! Heh, heh, heh, heh!

I'm sorry. *(Wipes mouth on sleeve.)* So this big dufus opens the door. Hey, Chonchi, have you noticed how there's always somebody like that guarding those places? Yup, that's what happens to you when you get too much bizcocho! I'm serious, yup, yup.

So we follows him up these green crickety velvety stairs with mirrors all around. That's so you don't feel so alone when you come to do your nasty thing. And when we get to the top, there is this fine, crazy-ill, superdope, lick-my-chops, to-die-for mami! Oh my God, she is ferocious!

What? You know Nilda? Okay then, I guess she wasn't such a mami. Okay, I guess she wasn't so ferocious. Okay, so she was more like this—this—this fat fat fat fat fat gargoyle with big tetas and shit.

But I says to her anyways, I says, "Excuse me, we'd like some mamis, please." And she says, "You're lookin' at her." So me and Ninja looks at each other, and we're both thinkin', "Naaaahhhh!" And she says, "It'll cost you thirty dollars each." Thirty dollars? For that? Well, all me and Ninja had was like five bucks between the two of us.

So I says to her, I says, "Excuse me, do you have somebody smaller?" And she says, "No, I'm all you need." And I says, "Fine, we'll come back next time and make reservations, all right?" And as we start to step, the big dufus grabs us, man. *(Reaches behind head and grabs shirt collar, standing on toes as if lifted from behind.)*

And she says, "I'mma take one of you anyway." So now me and Ninja got no choice but to choose. Odds—once, twice, three. . . . *(Shoots. Then, with false bravado.)* I won! Psych! Go Loco! Go Loco! Go Loco! Go Loco! *(Grooves, with fading enthusiasm.)* Well, actually I lost.

'Cause she takes me into this closet room with a mattress on the floor—and in a heartbeat she is butt-naked, man. And if she was fat then, she is triply colossal now! Yup, yup, she was like these—flaps! And these folds! *(Mimes.)* And these ripples and blobs of mocha ice cream stacked one on top of the other. She looked like this humongous caramel cloud!

And then she starts acting sexy and shit. *(Bats eyelashes and wiggles like a flirtatious young girl.)* Then she says to me, "I hope you're big! I hope you're real real real big!" Oh shit, Chonchi! That sent this ferocious bolt of fear to my Juanito Junior, you know what I'm saying? Like it almost climbed back inside of me. It was going, "Meep! Meep! Meep! Meep! Meep! Meep!" *(Whimpers and mimes the shriveling with finger.)*

Then she starts with, "Hurry, Papi! I want you. I want you now." So I start to take off my clothes real slow, hoping she'd get done by herself. *(Mimes.)* But uh-unh, she still going shtrong.

And when I gets to my BVDs, I peeps in *(peeps)*, and my red-helmeted warrior is in a coma! So I starts making with the apologies right away: "This never happened to me before, lady. I got a lot on my mind. I got personal problems, homework, world hunger on my mind."

But she don't care. She just reaches over and goes, "Cuchi cuchi cuchi!" *(Finger mimes tickling.)* And one-two-three—*(Klock noise with tongue.)* Se me paró! That's right! One body, two minds, what can I say? Ah hah! *(Cackles with bravado.)* So then she condomizes me, right? And I bless myself, just like my mother taught me before entering danger. *(Crosses himself.)* And I close my eyes. . . . *(With eyes closed, tries to find the edges of her body, reaching wider and wider.)* And I dives in.

Oh, Chonchi, man *(gyrates dreamily),* it is so soft . . . and warm . . . and plushhhh . . . that I begin humping like a maniac immediately. *(Wildly thrusts, arms still wide, eyes still closed.)* And she begins to laugh at me. So I begin to hump her a little more ferociously. And she laughs a little harder. So I really begin to drill her like a demon.

Well, now she's laughing so hard that she's almost crying, right. So I has to stop and ax her, "Excuse me, is it supposed to make you laugh like that?" And she says, "No, you got it in the wrong place!" *(Simulates Nilda's laughter.)* "*Hua, hua, hua!*" Oh my God, Chonchi, I felt just like I looked—stupid! I was lost in one of her flaps, man!

So what else could I do, but ax her, "Excuse me, could you please put me in the right place?" And she does. And oh my God, Chonchi man, if it was good then, it is heavenly now, boy! *(Closes eyes again.)* It is so gooey . . . and velvety . . . and safe. Then it hit me right there and then. I was born to fuck! I'm gonna fuck till I die and hopefully die fucking! And then I started to do all kinds of moves *(begins grooving and thrusting)* 'cause I saw it on Agamemnon's *Naked Personalities.* And she starts, "Ay, gracias, Papi! Gracias!" and her eyes roll right into the back of her head, and she begins to moan and groan. *(Groans à la Yosemite Sam.)* I thought she was going to die. But I can't stop myself, man. I'm on a mission. *(Thrusts rhythmically.)* I just keep going, and then one, two, three . . . *(Mimes orgasm with squish-squish-squish sounds.)* It's over. Just like that.

And I opens up my eyes—and she's this caramel soup! So I jump off her real quick, and I can't even look at her no more. And I do like the Santero said: *(mimes Santero ritual, brushing away spirits)* Pa' fuera, pa' fuera, pa' fuera, sucio demonio, coco inmundo, ayudame Diosito! And I shake all the evil away. I put on my clothes, and I'm outta there like a bullet, man—whoosh! I don't turn back.

I did it! I did it, man! I'm a man! I'm experienced! Aah! *(Crows and grooves.)* Go Loco! Go Loco! Go Loco! Go Loco! And here I am, Chonchi. I came to share my triumph with you, 'cause you are my homey.

(Suddenly serious, stammering.) But between you and me—'cause you're my homes—I was expecting my first time to be a little more . . . do you know what I'm saying? Like, I was hoping that it would be more . . . nah, it's not important. I'm a man now, and I don't gotta worry about shit like that no more.

Hey yo, Chonchi! You wanna be a man, too? My mom's got some money in her purse upstairs. Come on! Last one up is a dufus! I'll get you a discount, 'cause me and Nilda are tight like that now, boy. *(Crosses fingers.)* Let's bust a move! *(Turns on radio and begins dancing. Lights down.)*

ANGEL
GARCIA

*(Backstage lights up. A cell door clangs shut.
The silhouette of a handcuffed man is shoved
onstage.)* ANGEL GARCIA: Get your hands off
me, man! Get your hands off me! You're
hurting me! Get your rug-wearing fucking
guinea hands off me! Get the fuck off me.
You're trying to incarcetize me for something I
didn't do. *(A flash bulb pops offstage.)*

*(Rubs one handcuffed hand across nose; it
comes away bloody.)* Look at that! You broke
my nose, Desico! You didn't have to break my
nose, man. *(Another flash.)* I'm not an animal.
I'm a fucking human being! You got no
respect. . . . No, I'm not gonna go peaceably.
And speaking of piece, how's your wife?

(Comes downstage.) Yeah, yeah, Desico, spare me the Miranda. You have the right to remain stupid!

> *(Stage lights up as Angel turns to face the audience. He is wearing black jeans, a black leather jacket, open, with a T-shirt beneath, silver rings and bracelets, and an earring. His nose is bleeding profusely, all over his upper lip and chin, and his hands are bloody from wiping his face. The only props are a stool with a telephone on it, downstage.)*

(To audience:) Boo! What are you ass-snatchers staring at? Do you know me? I don't think so. What, you never seen someone busted before?

(Recognizes an inmate.) Hey, Ninja, is that you? Ninja Mutant Torres, what's a puto like you doin' in a fine institution like this? You can't even do your three-card monte right, stupid? . . . No, I didn't forget. We're in a recession, homes. I'm just trying to maximize my moneywise situation—then we'll agendicize. . . . Yeah, in your culo, puto maricón sucio.

(Pleadingly working the cop.) Desicoroonie, let me go, man! I swear I didn't do nothing. You're trying to incarcetize me for something I didn't do. I just had an argument with my woman, that's all. C'mon, you never disciplinify your women? I know you guidos, man. You're hot-headed just like we are.

Desico, I did not hit her! For your edification, I was just arguing with her, man—that's all. She had an accident. Come on, man—I love her! You know how much I love her? I was gonna breed with her. Now what does that tell you? . . . Well, your recollection does not matchesize with my recollection of the events.

(Confidential.) Check this out, Desico. Hear me out. I come home early, right? Boom. It's our anniversary, and I got some flowers, right? Boom. And I hear these suspicious noises,

right? I know what's going on, but I can't believe she's that stupid to play me like that. Boom. I open up the bathroom door, and she's got my homeboy on top of her. Boom, boom, boom! You see what I'm saying?

That's right, a special romantic other. What am I supposed to do—sit there and ref? That's my woman, man! I love her so much, I'm gonna kick her ass. *(Punches wall. Then, under his breath:)* I'm not gonna let it get to me. Nothing's gonna get to me.

(Turns and combs hair.) You think you're gonna get to me, Desico? I don't think so. You're just a pimple on my ass. A fart in the wind. You know what you are? Tú eres un mugre, un moco, una cucaracha. You see this? *(Spits.)* That's you. That's me. *(Points to exit.)* That's you. That's right. You couldn't even beat your own dick. Oh, you like that one, huh, Ninja? *(Tries to soothe furious cop.)* I wasn't dissin' you. I was just goofin'. That's the problem with you cops, you got no sense of humor.

(Spies phone.) C'mon, Desico, man. I know my rights. I got the right to call my people. Don't try to dispriviligize me, officeroonie. *(Plays to grab phone.)* Well, fuck you very much.

(Lifts receiver and dials. Wipes nose as he waits.) Hola, Negrito, how you doing, Papa? Are you all right? . . . No, I'm okay too. . . . No, Daddy can't tuck you in tonight, Papi. I got a lot of business to take care of. Could you go put your Mommy on the phone for me, please? . . . No, I don't want to talk to your dog. Just put Mommy on. . . . Okay, okay, okay. Woof, woof, woof. Now go put Mommy on, all right?

(Holds hand over mouthpiece and addresses the cop.) Desico, man, I'm going to be out of here faster than a virgin running from John Holmes.

(Back to phone.) What do you mean she's not home? Mira, I just heard her telling you to say she's not home! Tell her to get on the phone. . . . She doesn't want to talk to me? Negrito, put the phone up to Mommy. Go ahead, mijo. G'head.

ROSANNA, I KNOW YOU'RE THERE! YOU FUCKING DISRESPECTED ME! YOU SAY YOU'RE MINE, AND THEN YOU GO AND PLAY ME LIKE THAT? AFTER ALL I DID FOR YOU? YOU GET ON THAT PHONE RIGHT NOW!

She still doesn't want to talk to me? Okay then, Negrito, you know what you do? You go over and tell Mommy that it's her fault that Daddy's in jail. . . . No, Papa, don't tell her that. Tell her I'm sorry and that I love her and that my life is nothing without her—hello? Hello? Fucking stillborn, man! *(Slams receiver into cradle.)* Yeah, I should've drowned that little sucker when I had the chance, huh, Ninja?

(Wheedling.) Give me a chance, Desicoroonie. I won't charge it to you. Besides *(picks up receiver)* this black mami I'm calling is so fine, I would lick the dick of the last guy who fucked her just to get a taste of that papaya juice. *(Dials.)*

(Into phone.) Hello, Shanté? How you doin', Mami? . . . Oh, baby *(suave and seductive)*, you sound so good, I swear to God you do. You sound good enough to eat. . . . It's Angel. Angel Garcia. . . . The guy who wears the leopard jockeys? . . . Yeah, that Angel. That's better. Now listen, I'm in jail and I need you to post . . . No, not Yale. Jail! Jail! J-A-I . . . That's very funny. Tee-hee, tee-hee. Now come on, I don't have time to play games wichoo, all right? Listen, I need you to post bail for me at the hundred-tenth precinct. . . . Why not? . . . Oh, my God! I did not say "Rosanna, Rosanna" during sex. I

said . . . "Hosanna! Hosanna in the highest,"
in my big moment. I was just getting into it,
baby. You musta misfuckinunderstood. . . . I
didn't do no Rosanna. I don't even know a
Rosanna. . . . She called you? When?

Oh baby, oh woman. Oh, woman, please,
please, woman. . . . Listen, my little ebony
princess. Lovewise, I know I'm poison, okay? I
know I'm poison, Mami! Just 'cause a man
loves, doesn't mean he knows how to love. You
know, when I was born, my mother was in
labor for three days. Now what does that tell
you? . . . Yeah, even then I was causing
women pain. Go ahead and kick me when I'm
down! Go ahead and call me names if it'll make
you feel better. Express yourself.

*(Holds receiver away from ear, then tries to
calm her again.)* So, are you done? Are you
done? . . . No, I'll just wait here till you're
done, 'cause I got no place to go. . . . Listen,
woman! Listen! If you're talking, you're not
listening. . . . That's it! If I'm not out of here
by midnight, you're never gonna see me again,
and it's gonna be your fucking fault! . . .
Come on, baby, don't make me say shit I don't
mean. *(Turns upstage to keep cop from hearing
next lines.)* You know I love you. And that my
life is nothing without you. . . . Hello? Hello?

(To cop:) Hey, Desico, your phone's busted! I got cut off right in the middle of my conversation, man!

Come on, why you sweatin' me? Why you frontin' like that? I still haven't been connectitized. Give me a chance. *(Conspiratorial.)* I'll take care of you, I promise. I'll work something out. *(Threatening.)* Don't flex on me, 'cause I'll call my father and you'll find yourself hamburgerfied. Don't play me, 'cause I got more guts than a slaughterhouse. You'll find yourself wearing a concrete hat. I'll give you a Colombian necktie! *(Dials.)* Wrap that shit right around your neck, motherfuck—

(Into phone.) Hello? . . . Yeah, hello. Ah, can I speak to my mom, please? . . . No, man, I don't want to talk to you right now. Could you just put my mom on? . . . Are you deaf? I said I don't want to talk to you! . . . No, man, you're not my father. Just put her on!

Hola, Mamá, cómo esta? . . . Oh God, Mom, I'm so glad to hear your voice, you don't know! . . . It's your little Angel. . . . No, I don't want anything. Look, I'm just calling from the hundred-tenth precinct to see how you're doing, that's all! . . . Why you get so suspicious every time I call you?

Mom, are you drinking? *(Pain creeps into his voice.)* Oh—see—Ma, don't—don't do that drinking shit. You told me you weren't going to drink no more. . . . Well, then, stop listening to those stupid Julio Iglesias records if they make you cry. . . . All right, Mom, I'm going to be straight up with you. Yeah, I got into a little trouble. I hate to ask you, but can you come and get me at the hundred-tenth precinct? . . . I promise you I'll change. This is the last time. I swear this will never happen again. Now, can you just come down to the hundred-tenth precinct, please?

She called you? What did she say? . . . Don't
listen to her, Mom. I did not hit her, Mom.
She's a fucking liar, Mom! Don't believe
her. . . . Yeah, but did she tell you what she
did to me? . . . Okay, Mom, I don't have
time. I have a lot of business to take care
of. . . . Okay, okay, it'll never happen again, I
promise. Now can you just come down and get
me?

> Mom, no, don't put Grandma on now! Don't
> put— *(Sighs.)* . . . Hola, Abuelita, how you
> doin'? How's your hip? . . . Okay, could you
> put my mom back on, please? . . . Abuelita,
> the devil had nothing to do with it. . . . I
> don't really care what the Bible has to say, just
> put Mom back on. . . . What do you mean,
> God has the last laugh? What kind of thing is
> that to say to somebody? Get off the phone!

Mom, don't ever put her on again. Now can
you come down to the hundred-tenth precinct
and get me out of here? . . . It's like five stops
on the subway. . . . It's not dangerous, I take
the subway every fucking day! . . . I'm sorry,
I'll never curse again, all right? Just make that
asshole come with you!

It's the last time I'll ever ask anything of you again, I promise. I'm gonna change. . . . No, Mom, I gotta get out of here. . . . No, Mom, don't leave me here. *(Voice begins to crack as he becomes visibly upset.)* Don't listen to him. Why you always got to listen to him? Why don't you listen to me for a change? You owe me. You gave birth to me. . . . I don't care if I'm yelling at you, because you never cared for me, that's why! 'Cause the only time you fucking cared for me was when you had nobody else, that's when you fucking cared for me! . . . Oh, yeah, Ma, watchoo do for me? What? Let him beat me every fucking day of my life, is that what you did for me? *(Sighs.)* Now you're going to do that crying shit on me. You're going to do that crying shit.

(Holds receiver away and tries to compose himself.) Shh. Shh. . . . All right, Mom. Just forget it, okay? Don't come. . . . Yeah. I'll be fine. . . . No, I understand. Look, Mom, I got to go, okay? . . . Yeah, I know you love me. I know you love me. 'Bye. *(Almost hangs up, then puts phone back to his ear.)* Yo, Ma? . . . Yeah, if anything happens to me, it's gonna be your fault! *(Slams receiver down.)*

All right, Desico. Come on, man! *(Holds cuffed hands above his head.)* This is your big opportunity. So why don't you hurry up and lock me up, man?

I never needed nobody. 'Cause I got more guts than a slaughterhouse, that's why. Yo, Desico! You know what I want for breakfast, man? I want freshly squeezed OJ, I want Canadian bacon, and I want a Spanish omelette, man! That's right, I want you to make it nice and runny. I'm gonna Spanishify you, man!

I never needed nobody. *(Looks around.)* I could work this. I could work from here. I could definitely make this my office.

(Lights down.)

(The stage is dark. A backstage light reveals the silhouette of a man wearing jeans and a T-shirt standing in a doorway.)

PEPE: Excuse me, ése, I just got this gift certificate in the mail saying that I was entitled to gifts and prizes and possibly money if I came to La Guardia Airport? *(Comes downstage.)* Oh sure, the name is Pepe. Pepe Vásquez. *(Panics.)* Orale, what are you doing? You're making a big mistake! *(Lights up. Pepe stands center stage, holding a grille of prison bars in front of his face.)*

I'm not Mexican! I'm Swedish! No, you've never seen me before. Sure I look familiar—all Swedish people look alike. *(Gibberish in Swedish Accent.)* Uta Häagen, Häagen Däazen, Frusen Glädjé, Nina Häagen. . . .

Okay. Did I say Swedish? I meant Irish—yeah, black Irish! *(Singsongy Irish accent).* Toy ti-toy ti-toy. Oh, Lucky Charms, they're magically delicious! Pink hearts, green clovers, yellow moons. What time is it? Oh, Jesus, Joseph, and Mary! It's cabbage and corned beef time—let me go!

Okay. *(Confessional.)* You got me. I'm not Swedish and I'm not Irish. You probably guessed it already—I'm Israeli! Mazel tov, bubeleh *(Jackie Mason schtick.)* Come on, kine-ahora, open up the door. I'll walk out, you'll lock the door, you won't miss me, I'll send you a postcard. . . .

Orale, gabacho pendejo. I'm American, man. I was born right here in Flushing. Well, sure I sound Mexican. I was raised by a Mexican nanny. Doesn't everybody have a Maria Consuelo?

As a matter of fact, I got proof right here that I'm American. I got two tickets to the Mets game. Yeah, Gooden's pitching. Come on, I'm late.

Orale, ése. Is it money? It's always money. *(Conspiratorially.)* Well, I got a lot of money. I just don't have it on me. But I know where to get it.

Orale, ése. Tell me, where did your people come from? Santo Domingo? Orale, we're related! We're cousins! Tell me, what's your last name? Rivera? Rivera! That's my mother's maiden name! What a coinky dinky. Hermano, cousin, brother, primo, por favor dejeme ir que somos de la mismita sangre. Los latinos debemos ser unidos y jamás seremos vencidos.

Oh, you don't understand, huh? You're a coconut. *(Angry.)* Brown on the outside, but white on the inside. Why don't you do something for your people for a change and let me out of here?

Okay, I'm sorry, cuz. *(Apologetic.)* Come here. Mira, mijito, I got all my family here. I got my wife and daughter. And my daughter, she's in the hospital. She's a preemie with double pneumonia and asthma. And if you deport me, who's gonna take care of my little chucawala?

Come on, ése. It's not like I'm stealing or living off of you good people's taxes. I'm doing the shit jobs that Americans don't want. *(Anger builds again.)* Tell me, who the hell wants to work for two twenty-five an hour picking toxic pesticide-coated grapes? I'll give you a tip: Don't eat them.

Orale, you Americans act like you own this place, but we were here first. That's right, the Spaniards were here first. Ponce de León, Cortés, Vásquez, Cabeza de Vaca. If it's not true, then how come your country has all our names? Florida, California, Nevada, Arizona, Las Vegas, Los Angeles, San Bernardino, San Antonio, Santa Fe, Nueva York!

Tell you what I'm going to do. I'll let you stay
if you let me go.

What are you so afraid of? I'm not a threat. I'm
just here for the same reason that all your
people came here for—in search of a better life,
that's all.

(Leans away from grille, then comes back
outraged.) Okay, go ahead and send me back.
But who's going to clean for you? Because if we
all stopped cleaning and said "adiós," we'd still
be the same people, but you'd be dirty! Who's
going to pick your chef salads? And who's
going to make your guacamole? You need us
more than we need you. 'Cause we're here
revitalizing the American labor force!

Go ahead and try to keep us back. Because
we're going to multiply and multiply (thrusts
hips) so uncontrollably till we push you so far
up, you'll be living in Canada! Oh, scary
monsters, huh? You might have to learn a
second language. Oh, the horror!

But don't worry, we won't deport you. We'll just let you clean our toilets. Yeah, we don't even hold grudges—we'll let you use rubber gloves.

Orale, I'm gonna miss you white people.

(Lights down.)

MANNY THE FANNY

*(Dance music plays. Backstage light silhouettes
Manny, voguing seductively. Music fades. A
figure appears and drags her onstage. Manny
has long orange hair and shiny lipstick to
match. She wears a skin-tight hot-pink
minidress, black patent-leather pumps,
doorknocker earrings, and large jangly
bracelets; has Walkman headphones around her
neck; and carries a black evening bag.)*

MANNY THE FANNY *(to figure:)* I didn't
come here to eat your food. I wouldn't eat at
Chez Greasy Spoon if it was the last food on
earth! Whaddya think, this establishment's
exclusive? I just came here to take a piss!

(Lights up.) Don't talk to me like that, you old
pervert. 'Cause I'll read you from cover to
cover and you'll never recover. *(Snaps.)*

You people come here, you gentrify the neighborhood, you kick us out, and then you won't let us use the bathroom? You can kiss my amber ass. *(Sticks ass out.)* Go ahead and kiss it. Kiss it. Kiss it! I dare you. . . . Don't you dare, 'cause I'll come over there and slice your motherfucking pipi off! *(Pulls giant knife from purse.)* Te lo corto. I'm not playing wichoo.

(Moves toward audience. Yells to nearby cops.) Mira, mira! Policía, policía, please! Ayuda, socorro, socorro! There's a case of discrimination going on over here.

Well, shit, I would if you had one! Oink, oink, oink—oops! Perdóna, señor policía! I'm just playing wichoo.

Well, don't give me that butch look. Save it for the cow at home! Oops—was that me? Did I say that? Ay, perdóna. This girl's got a big mouth, but she knows how to use it! *(Snaps three times in the sign of Zorro.)* Chaito, señor policía. *(Blows kiss to departing cops.)* Baboso.

I gotta do número uno real bad. I need a date, I need a date! *(Spots potential customer.)* Mira, Papi! Papi . . . *(indignant)* Baboso!

(Sings and vogues.)

> Girlfriend, how could you let him treat you
>   so bad?
> Girlfriend, you know you are the best thing
>   he ever had. . . .

> *(Spies another potential customer.)* Csst, csst,
> csst *(as for dog)*. *(Blows kiss and acts
> seductive.)* Ay, mira, precioso, mind if I say
> *wow*! Why don't you stop and say hello? I'm
> like white chocolate—none of the color, but all
> of the flavor! You're not from around here.
> Where you from? . . . Milwaukee? Ooh, I like
> foreigners! Do you have a bathroom in your
> hotel? . . . Then why don't you let Manny the
> Fanny show you a good time?

Well, excuse me, your royal blackness!
(Curtsies.) Stuck-up latent homosexual! Fuck
you, your daddy is a faggot and he likes it. I
know—I had him! *(Snaps both hands.)* Go
ahead, throw that bottle. But you better have
good aim, 'cause if I'm not dead *(pulls knife
from purse),* I'm gonna come over there and
slice your motherfucking pipi off! *(Mimes.)* I'm
not playing wichoo.

> *(Vogues and sings; spies friend down the
> street.)* Csst, csst, csst, csst! *(Then very loud:)*
> PSSSSSSST! *(Stomps foot and screams.)*

Rosanna! *(Snaps three times.)* Rosanna! Mira, Rosanna, you flat-chested no-ass spicarella! You hear me calling you. Don't pretend you don't know me, girl. What do I look like, a hologram? You must have flunked your manners at the Copacabana School of Etiquette, Miss Très Beaucoup Faux Pas! *(Snaps.)*

What are you doing on this side of the planet, nena? I'm so glad to see you. I got so much to tell you! Last night I met this papi. Ay, he was bien de groovy, tú sabes? Casi que me muero.

What's a matter wichoo? Oh girl, you're always down. Don't tell me, I know—a terrible thing happened to you again last night. Nothing! Ouch! Ha, ha! *(Snaps and twirls.)* I'm sorry.

You know I'm cold-blooded. So malicious
(snap) and delicious! *(Snap.)*

Look at me when I talk to you. Don't cover
your face. Come on, what's a matter wichoo?

Ay! Dios mío! Ay, no. *(Cringes, hand to heart.)*
I didn't know. I swear to God I didn't know.
Bendito, poor fragile thing. Okay, take a deep
breath and pull your sorry self together.

Qué te pasó? What happened to you? Rosanna,
if you can't talk to me, who can you talk to?
Angel did that to you? Ay, nena, you can't let
my brother beat you like that. That no-good
low-life with his forty-deuce mentality and
Delancey Street sales pitch! I'd like to hurt him.
I'd like to cut his motherfucking pipi off for
you! *(Takes a deep breath.)* Ay, Dios mío. Look
at you. You look like you got hit by a truck—
and you weren't that good-looking to begin
with, neither!

Ay, listen to me. Ay, fo! Mira, nena, I know
exactly what you are going through, because I
have been there myself. I was a pendeja too. A
regular little Miss Masoquista. Just like those
poor sick bitches you see across the street. *(To*

women across street:) Yes, I'm talking to you! Ho! *(To Rosanna:)* Always hooked up with abusive pricks, that was moi. Because I thought getting slapped around and getting kicked upside my head was better than nothing, as long as there was somebody in my bed when I woke up in the morning. Because somewhere in this warped mind of mine, I just convinced myself that it was love. And from then on I was lost en el mundo de "cheap thrills y expensive regrets," tú sabes? Oh, don't go. 'Cause let me tell you, it gets even worse!

One day, I met this one dark prince. This guy who played me like a fine violin. Plucked my G-string just right and made me feel like everything was Disney. And this poor sick puppy put all of herself into this one guy, 'cause she heard wedding bells. So I gave him all my money, pawned all my possessions, and gave up a once-promising career as a cosmetologist at the Wilfred Academy of Beauté *(snaps)* just to send this Judas hijo de puta through night school.

But unbeknownst to me, he was just using me and taking all my money to entertain other bimbettes and laughing—laughing, mind you—at this poor lovesick freak behind her back. *(Sighs.)* But when I caught wind—and let me tell you, I did—Sleeping Beauty awoke! *(Cross snaps.)*

So, I came home early one night and I unscrewed all the bulbs *(mimes)* and hid in the closet with an iron in one hand and Krazy Glue en la otra. *(Mimes, eyes closed.)* And I waited.

Nine o'clock . . . ten o'clock . . . eleven o'clock . . . I thought he was never gonna come, right? But at exactly midnight, in sashays the Judas hijo de puta. Trying to turn the lights on and calling my name all lovey-dovey: "Oh, Manny? Manny, I got something for you. I got something for you." I got something for you, too, cabrón! And I just held my breath, 'cause this girl wasn't about to let his magic wand cast a spell on her again.

Then I heard his Florsheims get closer—and closer—and closer—and when he got to the closet door, I prayed for God to give me the strength and I popped out and conked him on the head with the iron. And on his way down, I undid his zipper, took out his big ol' pinga, put Krazy Glue up and down, and slapped it to his thigh. *(Mimes ever so daintily.)* Then I dragged the body out and locked the door. *(Wipes hands.)* Punishment accomplished, right! *(Snaps.)*

But when he came to—ay, Dios mío! He was screaming and crying, "I'm going to get you,

Manny! I'm going to kill you! I'm going to beat you to death!" I knew then I'd done something wrong. *(Bites finger.)* But I didn't care no more. And do you know why, nena? *(Empowered.)* Because I took charge of my life. So I just flicked on the radio and drowned him out. *(Jumps into a routine.)*

To be or not to be,
That is the question.
You've lied your last lie *(hands talk)*
And I've cried my last cry. *(Wipes tear.)*
You're out the door, baby! *(Points out and locks the door.)*
There's other fish in the sea. *(Reels in fish.)*
Olé! *(Grand finale of snaps.)*

So, you see what I'm telling you? Oh, I know I'm crazy. *(Tenderly.)* But life is too short to let people crush your world. But yo te conozco. I know you, Rosanna. You'll go home and he'll beat you and you'll let him beat you and you'll go through this love-hate hate-love thing till one day you're hiding in the closet with an iron in one hand and Krazy Glue en la otra.

But until that day, don't live on dreams. Because there are no Prince Charmings coming to save you. Just a lot of frogs. So you know what you do? You take your frog by his little green dick and you make him do what *you* wanna do. Because you are a Latina of the nineties. *(Snaps.)* Get with the program, mija! If it wasn't for a Spanish woman, Columbus woulda never discovered America. *(Double snap.)* Olé!

Now go ahead and get home before he beats you up for breathing. Take care of yourself, nenita. And call me. Call me, I'll get the message. Call me at Nilda's. Yeah, 'cause she wants me to play a practical joke on this little boy named Loco. *(Blows kiss.)* Chaito.

(Alone. Looks skyward.) Oh God, please take care of her. *(Sings and vogues.)* Girlfriend, why do you let him treat you so bad? Girlfriend . . . ay, Dios mío. I need to do número uno so bad, I can taste it—please! *(Sucks in breath.)* Ay, Dios mío, I need a date. I need a date.

(Spies guy in midaudience.) Csst, csst, csst, csst, csst! *(Blows sexy kiss. Advances toward audience.)* Ay, mira, precioso, mind if I say *wow*!

(Lights down.)

INCA PRINCE

(Backstage lights up. Latin music plays. A man and a woman are in silhouette. He takes her arm.) INCA PRINCE: Come on, baby, let's go upstairs. . . . What's the matter? I didn't go messin' around. I was just out drinkin' with the fellas. Come on, I'm gonna take you to paradise, baby. . . . What? He's cryin'? What's he cryin' about? . . . All right. All right, I'll go talk to him. Stop bustin' my onions. Just go upstairs and wait for me. *(Stage lights up. Inca Prince enters, drunk. He wears a white tank top, jeans, and a bandana on his head with an Aztec medallion on the forehead. He weaves toward a small bed downstage.)* What do you mean I'm not gonna get any? Is that a threat or a promise? It wouldn't be the first time.

(To child in the bed:) Come on, Carlitos, I know you're not sleepin'—stop pretendin'. I wanna talk to you. Your mother isn't going to wait for me forever.

(Turns and shouts out window.) Hey, turn that goddamn music down! People are trying to sleep up here! *(Music gets louder.)* Ever since those goddamn Colombians moved in, nobody can get any sleep!

(Sits on the edge of the bed and addresses the child.) You're crying. What are you crying about? I got something for you. *(Pulls out Spiderman toy and sings.)* Spiderman, Spiderman . . . does whatever a spider can. Catches thieves just like flies, here comes the spider man. *(Plays with toy trying to get Carlitos's attention. The kid doesn't respond.)* I tried.

Why are you crying? . . . They called you a name? That's why you're crying? Don't you ever let me hear that somebody called you names and you didn't beat the motha! I taught you how to defend yourself. I taught you how to box. Do I have a son, or do I have a little daughter?

(Playful—almost trying to make up for what he just said.) You got nothing to be ashamed of. Don't you know you are a direct descendant of the raven-eyed Inca god, Chibcha? Hark! We have the spirits of the ancients in our blood! You think I'm just a bum with an Incan headdress, but you're wrong. I am authentic, seriously authentic. I'm the santero mágico, the magic man!

(Really hams it up, trying to make the boy laugh.) Oh, wait a minute—I'm getting a communication from above. Hmmm. What is that, O Great One? Hmmm. I should what? . . . Slow down—too much info. . . . I should offer the world-secret lotion notion potion *(pulls bottle of booze from back pocket)* to this mortal? To this puny little mortal? This must be your lucky day, Carlitos! This potion was obtained by my great-great-great-cousin Julio La Brea Cahuenga Tahunga La Cienagea something or other. He was the great Aztec thief. All you have to do is give a little of this to the woman you crave, and she will perform the most unnatural and uncomfortable acts you want. You'll appreciate this when you get a little older. *(Takes a swig.)*

We come from so many famous people, Carlitos. People who have done this and done that. . . . Like who? Like who. Like Maria

Consuelo Cleopatra. . . . What, you didn't know she was Latina? Sure—as a matter of fact, Marc Antonio Rodríguez was madly in love with her.

And how about Guilliam Shakesperez? Yeah, Guilliam Shakesperez. He wrote some great stuff— *Romero y Julieta, Macho Do About Nothing, The Merchant of Venice-Zuela.* "Alas, alack, alook and a lick, hither, thither, fie, fie, fie. . . ." You didn't know he was a quarter Latino? Oh, yeah. As a matter a fact, inside of every great person there's always a little Latino.

(Pointing bottle at Carlitos.) Hey, pay attention! 'Cause this is for your benefit. I already know this shit.

(Pulls bottle away from kid.) No, you can't have any. When you work hard all day at a job you don't like and are married and have kids, then you can drink all you want.

What did you call me? Don't worry, I'm not gonna hit you—I wanna know what you called me. . . . Don't you ever talk to me like that.

You respect me! I'm your father! . . . Is that what they called me? Is that what you're crying about? Well, tomorrow I'm gonna go to school with you and you're gonna tell all your little friends that I'm the most famous has-been, coulda-been, woulda-been that they ever gonna meet.

(Stands up and mimes sportscaster, using bottle as mike and speaking in a booming voice.) In this corner, all the way from Avenue A, the undefeated lightweight champion of the Loisaida *(he flexes and poses)*, the Inca Prince. Yeah! Yeah! *(As crowd would cheer. Then in normal voice.)* The babes tingled. The men admired me. I was handsome and sleek and in my prime. *(Poses bodybuilder style.)* The most powerful hands known to mankind.

I fought for the championship, Carlitos. We came at each other like two wild dogs. Left, right, left. *(Mimes.)* The first punch—I knew I had him. I knew I had him! By the end of the fifth, I came at him with everything. The crowd was roarin' for me! Upper cuts, combos, the whole nine.

When he went to his corner, I heard him say, "I don't know, Dad, but every time he hits me, it paralyzes me. It feels like his gloves are full of rocks!"

Of course it does, because I'm the Inca Prince. Yeah! I made his face look like raw meat. Knocked him and his father's dreams right out. *(Lunges.)*

At the end of the bout the ref comes over to shake my hand and takes my gloves and squeezes. *(More sober.)* He found the little rips, the little tears, and the missing padding. He took the fight away from me. It was mine, and he took it away from me. I could have won that fight on my own, but I thought, the sure thing, always go for the sure thing. I made a mistake—a big mistake—on the biggest night of my life. *(Primordial scream.)*

(Turns to Carlitos.) What's that? That's right. Spiderman, Spiderman—does whatever a spider can. Catches thieves. . . . You know, Carlitos, when I was a puny kid just like yourself Spiderman was my biggest hero. Because he was just like me. Short, broke, but he had that Spidey sense and no one could touch him. And I used to pray all the time that when he took off that mask and costume, there'd be this little Spanish man in there. Of course, there never was.

So believe in yourself, because they can knock you down, but they can't knock you out. I love you, Carlitos, and that's the best I can give you. But if you don't go to sleep, I'm going to give you a big cocotazo. Good night, little Inca Prince.

(To offstage:) I'm coming, woman. If you can't wait, then why don't you start without me?

(Lights down.)

CROSSOVER KING

(Japanese gong sounds. Audience sees silhouette of a man doing a low bow. Lights up as the Crossover King enters from behind the scrim. He wears a conservative gray suit, white shirt, muted silk tie, silk hanky in breast pocket, wing tips, and thick black-framed glasses, and he carries notes. His hair is slicked back and his movements are controlled. He walks to the lectern, center stage, and places the notes on the stand, beside a full glass of water. When he speaks—in a Japanese accent—his gestures are stiff. He pushes the bridge of his glasses with his index finger.)

CROSSOVER KING: Oh, yes, you in the right place. *(Arranges notes.)* The Crossover Seminar is about to begin, so hurry up and grab a seat. Hai! *(Violently bows head as he exclaims. Sips water.)*

Konichi-wa. Dozo ohairi kudusai.
Hai! *(Jerks head.)* Welcome and
welcome, Latino-sans, to the Crossover
Seminar. Now, this could very well be the
biggest investment of your entire life, so please
hold your questions until the end. Hai! *(Jerks
head, then sips water.)*

You too could be a crossover success. It's up to
you *(points to an audience member)* and you
(points to another). This is purely a scientific
method. There are no placebos or messy
ointments.

Now, what exactly is a crossing over, you ask?
That's a good question. Crossing over is the art
of passing for someone that you are not in
order to get something that you have not.
Because there is no room in the corporate
upscale world for flamboyant, fun-loving spicy
people. So get used to it. I did.

Let's talk about the American mind made simple. Americans admire what? . . . Don't all volunteer at once. I have all day. . . . Am I speaking a foreign language? Americans admire what? I'll give you a hint: It's green, you used to be able to buy things with it. *(Answer from audience: "Money.")* Arrigato! She is ready for the advanced course, but the rest of you have to stay. Yes, Americans admire money, but they also admire the appearance of having money. The more money you have, the more respect you're going to get. But if you can't have the money, you sure better look like you have it. Because America keeps sending you the subliminal and not-so-subliminal signals that without money you are inadequate.

Stop. *(Hits himself on the head.)* Stop hitting yourselves in the head and think for a moment. Why settle for being Latin trash? Why even settle for being American trash, when you could be so much more? So much more—like Japanese! This is a rich market to be harvested, Latino-sans. You alone have the choice: American *(holds right hand low, by hip)* . . . Japanese *(holds left hand high in the air)* . . . Japanese . . . American . . . good . . . bad . . . bad . . . good. You choose. Hai! *(Jerks head.)*

I'm going to share a little secret with you. You won't believe this *(confessional)*, but I was a Latino-san myself. *(Visibly ashamed.)* Yes, it's true. But with this easy-to-follow program, I have evolved and become a Japanese warrior. Very repressed, but also very successful.

I used to be loud and obnoxious, full of street mannerisms. Constantly holding my crotch for self-assurance. *(Mimes awkwardly.)* I would yell all the time, "Hola, Ramón! I just had a girl with tetas to here and culo out to there!" *(Mimes.)* But now I zen-out and only speak when I have something really important to say.

I used to not even be able to walk down the street and hear rhythmic percussion without my hips beginning to gyrate wildly and uncontrollably. *(Hips gyrate beneath lectern.)* But now I listen to Lite FM. And I hardly move at all—even when I want to. *(Sips water.)*

I used to be full of Latino macho braggadocio, disrespecting my women and wanting to start fights all the time. *(Picks audience member.)* Watchoo looking at? Watchoo looking at? You talking to me? You talking to me? *(Steps out from behind lectern.)* I'll sucker-punch you, head-butt you, body-slam you, knock you to the ground, and spit in your eye. *(Suddenly all*

business again.) Et cetera, et cetera, et cetera.
(Returns to lectern.) Relax. It was just a
dramatic re-creation. Hai! *(Jerks head.)*

But no more. Now all my aggression goes into
beating up my business partners.

I know, a lot of you are thinking, "I don't need
this. I don't see anything wrong with me. I like
the way I am." Fine—but nobody cares what
you think. It's what *they* think that counts.

(Sets up a projection screen.) Now, I'm going to
accompany myself with some visual aids in
order to more closely examine these cases of

traditional stereotypicality. If you recognize yourself or loved ones, please do not panic. The Crossover King is here. Hai! *(Picks up projector remote from downstage.)* This is not for the squeamish, so be brave, Latino-sans, and face up.

Now, is your hair bleached to a color not found in nature? These are my cousins, the Henna sisters: Lizette, Annette, and Jeanette. They have a henna dependency from trying to be blonde sexy mamis. But I put them on a detox program, and I'm slowly easing them off the dyes and peroxides.

*Identities have been obscured to protect the unfortunate.

Do you wear Fourteenth Street doorknocker earrings, like my little sister, Yolanda? Those are dangerous! A big wind could come and knock her out and kill her. And you'd have another doorknocker-related death.

Do you make the streets your office?

Our photographer took this shot two weeks later and Miss Guzman was still there. Please get a life, Miss Guzman.

Oh, this is a special case. *(Ceremoniously takes collapsible pointer from breast pocket and unfolds it; uses to illustrate specific features on remaining slides.)* Are your clothes cutting off your circulation? Might you have the Aztec curse? *(To slide:)* Yes, Angela, you know what I'm talking about.

Guacamole hips.

Those arroz con pollo thighs.

Big ol' cuchifrito butt.

Look at that panty line.

The dreaded
tortilla chins.

How many can you count? *(Uses pointer to count off at least four chins, then advances to black slide.)*

If you have developed any of these characteristics, you may have already become what Americans call, behind your back, the little, brown, roly-poly, Spanish, submissive, subservient, no-good Latina puta-bitch! Now let's not help perpetuate negative stereotypes. Only you can prevent this ugly misrepresentation.

I know some of you are thinking, "That's all very well and good, but what can that Crossover King really do for me? What is that little devil up to?" Stay with me.

Here we have my aunt, Rosa Herrera. She was
a loud, gum-snapping, hairy-lipped, Bacardi-
drinking, welfare-leeching, child-bearing,
underachieving, no-good Latina puta-bitch. Oh,
she was so loud! She would talk your head off
all the time: "Did you see so-and-so? She's
pregnant again. He'll never marry her now.
Why buy the cow when you can get the milk
for free? Blah, blah, blah. Yak, yak, yak."

But with our program, Rosa Herrera has become . . .

Rose Hara, the timid, self-disciplined, lonely, constipated workaholic. Her hair is a human color. No makeup to make her look like some exotic tropical fish. No American don't-push-me-I-get-paid-by-the-hour attitude. From head to toe she is a model of respectability. Why, she could attend a party at a Tokyo Hilton and not even be told that the servants' entrance is in back. She has crossed over nicely. Hai!

Now for you men—or homeys, as you like to be called—don't think I was going to forget you. I suggest you take special note. Awareness is the first step to self-improvement.

This is my cousin Hector, the drug dealer. Oh yes, he is hard and tough—but so are arithmetic and calculus!

Look at all that gold.

It is better invested in a money market account than hung around his nefarious neck.

This is Tito Testosterones. He beat me up in the seventh grade—because I knew who my father was. Tito is the typical greasy, catfish-mustachioed, fake-gold-chain-wearing, beeper-carrying, polyester-loving, untrustworthy, horny, uncircumcised spic specimen. He will never get anywhere, except in a lineup.

(Addresses slide.) Look at me, Tito. Look at this success story now. *(Uses pointer on himself.)* Savile Row worsted tweed, Sulka Sulka tie, Varnet frames, Gucci shoes, Fortune-500 Ivy Leaguer that I've become. *(Turns to slide again, agitated.)* Look at me, Tito. I said look at me. *(Loses control completely.)* Cabrón, idiota, medio-malparido, cagado, pedazo de mierda envuelto, baboso, bobo. . . . *(Struggles to regain composure.)* Shitsurei. *(Bows.)* Shitsurei. *(Bows.)* Excuse me. This never happened to me before. I had a little Latino relapse. *(Straightens clothes, smooths hair.)*

But our expert computer graphics team suggests
that with only six months in our program, Tito
could become . . .

Toshino, the quiet one! Well-dressed,
manicured, somewhat anal retentive, but an
overachiever who's ready to enter the job
market at a drop of the value of the dollar.
*(Clicks slides off and deposits remote
downstage, then returns to lectern.)*

Once you have dulled your personality and have become lifeless and unimaginative, you are ready to reap the rewards of the corporate world. Don't wait for miracles. All it takes is a lot of restraint and a little bit of Japanese know-how.

(Incensed.) Now, I'm your Crossover King, and I'm going to help you to cross over. And if you don't like it, you can just kiss my yellow tail. Yes, I said it. Because we are going to own everything anyway. We are going to own your mother, your father, everybody, so you better cross over while you still can. It's nothing personal, just big business. And we're going to take all our competition, and we're going to sucker-punch them, head-butt them, body-slam them. . . . *(Shakes, sweats, and begins to fall apart.)* Ay coño, yo quiero perder control, ser lo que soy. . . . ayudame, mamacita, estoy jodido, quiero bailar y gozar . . . *(Becomes completely unhinged, conking, tearing open shirt, and spewing forth a torrent of Spanish profanity.)*

(Tries desperately to control himself, clinging to lectern, and is finally able to gulp down some water. Pants and sweats.) Just kidding. Just kidding, like you American people say, just kidding. Well, being Latino need not be a handicap. Don't settle for affirmative action

and tokenism. *(His feet begin mambo dancing beneath the lectern, while the rest of his body tries to hold still.)* Purge yourself of all ethnicity. *(His dancing feet take him out from behind the lectern. His upper body is still stiff.)* Well, that's all the time we have for tonight. Thank you for attending. *(Tries to control his legs, slaps his thighs.)* Remember, all it takes is a lot of restraint and a little . . . *(Bursts.)* Go Loco! Go Loco! Go Loco! *(Grooves.)*

Sayonara. Hai! *(Deep bow to audience.)*

(Lights down.)

ABOUT THE AUTHOR

JOHN LEGUIZAMO, as writer and performer, received critical acclaim and won the 1991 Obie and Outer Critics Circle awards for his first one-man show, *Mambo Mouth*. He obtained the 1992 Lucille Lortel Award for Best Actor in an Off-Broadway Play for his second, *Spic-O-Rama,* which won the Dramatists Guild's Hull-Warriner Award for Best Play of 1992. Both have been broadcast on HBO and the film version of *Mambo Mouth* received four ACE nominations.

Raised in Jackson Heights, Queens, Leguizamo studied drama at New York University, where he appeared in the award-winning student film *Five Out of Six*. He made his television debut as Calderon Jr. in *Miami Vice* and went on to appear in the films *Casualties of War, Revenge, Hangin' with the Homeboys,* and *Whispers in the Dark*. He co-stars in *Super Mario Brothers* with Bob Hoskins and Dennis Hopper, in *Carlito's Way* with Al Pacino and Sean Penn, and in the forthcoming buddy film *Nothing to Lose*. He is currently writing his first screenplay, *White Chocolate,* with Peter Askin, as well as a television comedy special, *House of Buggin'*.